5 Minute Classroom Manager

5 Minute Classroom Manager

Behavior in a Nutshell

Dr. Roberta Silfen

To order additional copies of this book, contact:
Xlibris Corporation
1-888-795-4274
www.Xlibris.com
Orders@Xlibris.com
101558

CONTENTS

Introduction

The following pages provide techniques for managing students exhibiting disruptive behaviors in the classroom.

Each group of activities are an outgrowth of a specific theory for changing behavior. You will find one or more compatible with your specific personality. Choose the one which you feel most comfortable with and begin. They all work—the key to success is perseverance and consistency on your part.

You will be providing the students with the opportunity to learn how to change their behavior as well as be responsible for their own behaviors. The students will become socially acceptable positive contributors in the classroom as they build their self-esteem.

Behavior Modification—Reinforcing Behavior

I. Theory—Attention is a reinforcing stimulus.
   A. If you ignore a behavior it decreases in frequency and eventually disappears.
   B. If you attend to a behavior, it increases in frequency.
   C. Therefore –   1. Reinforce positive behavior.
                    2. Ignore negative behavior.

II. Reinforcement Systems
   A. Token Reinforcement
      1. Reinforcing with tokens, tickets, stars, etc. to be exchanged for other things (tangibles).
      2. Other tokens or rewards – material reinforcers
         a. candy
         b. throw away toys
      3. Non-material reinforcers
         a. free-time after work completed
         b. play a game in class

III. Time for Reinforcement
   Immediately after a positive behavior is exhibited.
   A. Start with smaller units (class period) increase to a morning/ afternoon and eventually an entire day.
   B. As soon as a negative behavior is replaced by a positive one by one student, recognition will increase its occurrence. (A child who shouts out in class, ignore this behavior. When the child finally raises his hand, make sure you call on him and do so each time he raises his hand, he will stop calling out).

Behavior Modification—Conditioning

1. Operant Conditioning—Skinner
2. Shaping New Behavior—Pavlov
3. Counterconditioning designed to change behavior—Wolpe

There are 2 types of behavior:

A. Adaptive—desirable
B. Maladaptive—undesirable
1. Both types are developed and maintained by reward (positive reinforcement) from the environment in ways that are immediate and observable.
2. Current behavior is the result of many kinds of experiences children have had with significant others who have the power to reward and punish their behavior.
   a. You determine the behavior you want to extinguish and what you want to replace it with.
   b. You tell the child this and how you will proceed (ignore misbehaviors, reward good behaviors).
*3. My opinion – If you tell them, they may try to test you to see just how much of the misbehavior you will actually ignore, and it may get much worse. I prefer not to say anything to the child but first proceed to ignore the misbehaviors and reward the positive behavior. At the end of the class period you may pull the child aside and say "I like the way you raised your hand in class today when you wanted to say something."

Contingency Management

I. Theory—If a child can exhibit one activity (desirable) for a specific period of time, then you permit a short time for a reinforcing activity. YOU SPECIFY THIS TO THE CHILD.

    A. "If you sit quietly and do . . . . then you may . . . (run in place or . . for . . .) or until the timer goes ding."

    B. Teacher needs to find which behaviors are reinforcing to the child.
   1. Going to the restroom.
   2. Using paints/crayons.
   3. Listening to a tape.
   4. Using the computer.
   5. Pushing a rolling chair around the room.
   6. Emptying the trash can.
   7. Erasing the chalkboard.
   8. Getting a drink of water.
   9. Wearing sunglasses in the class.

    All the above should be specified beforehand.

    C. Other Activities
   1. If you have "time-out" and the child is to sit quietly – at the end of the timeout praise the child for sitting quietly.
   2. Vary the time for an instructional activity for a child to be successful. Start out with a short period – when you know the child can sit still for that length of time – then praise child for doing it. Lengthen slowly by increments (no more than 2 minutes a week).
   3. As mentioned previously—tokens given when children on task. Teacher goes around room leaves a token on desk of child on task. Doesn't mention it – just does it. If a child say "I did this and so can I have a token?" this is ignored. Teacher watches for appropriate behavior and when presented can reinforce with "good, you're doing fine," "keep it up." Tokens can be used to purchase

special event tickets (12-20 tokens can equal a special event). A student can accumulate 15 tokens a day.

Special events can be snacks, leaving the room for a special purpose, allowed to sit in a corner and read etc.

D. Variations

    1. For Peer Pressure Control—give rewards by groups working—peers control behavior of others.

    2. Increase length of time gradually for tokens.

    3. Increase amount of tokens needed (gradually 1 for a special event).

    4. Set up store in the classroom that children can exchange tokens for:

        a. candy, gum, balloons, baseball cards.

        b. comics.

        c. opportunity to write poetry on the computer.

        d. a model airplane.

        e. a science project.

        f. give a child the right to select his own curriculum for a part of the school day (offer choices).

Extinction—Counterconditioning

I. Theory—To cause a behavior to become extinct, you withhold the reinforcement that has previously maintained it, while the behavior is in evidence. You only provide positive reinforcement when acceptable behavior is presented.

   A. Example – a student develops a disturbing whistling sound which is maintained by attention. Teacher may stop speaking or give no attention to the whistling behavior. When the whistling stops the teacher recognizes it by saying "Very good, now we can go ahead."

   B. Above example could cause the child to start again in order to get attention when he stops – this can be avoided by:

      1. Don't reinforce the cessation immediately – otherwise you are rewarding cessation.

      2. If it doesn't start again – reinforce the child a number of times during the class period.

II. Other Activities – Group Peer Pressure

      1. Inform students there will be a 10 minute recess period at the end of the day when they can play a game, talk to friends etc. However, if there are disruptions by students during the day, they will have 1 minute less of recess whenever or each time this happens.

         You can start each day with a #10 on the board and minus sign next to it – when there's a disruption put a tally mark – no discussion each time. They will be able to keep track of their time themselves.

      2. Make sure you give them the time at the end of each day.

   *3. If they never get the time, they'll never improve behavior – you may have to adjust your behavior as to what you take minutes away for – to be sure they eventually get some recess time.

How To Use A Token System

Token Systems of reinforcement are implemented when social reinforcers such as teacher praise and approval have been ineffective in controlling the behavior of children.

I.   Effective—because they involve the presentation of a token following a specific response. When the child accumulates a sufficient number of tokens, he can exchange them for "back up" reinforcers (candy etc.). The tokens are initially "neutral" stimuli which become reinforcers because they can be exchanged for tangibles. Teacher praise and approval are often paired with tokens – in order to increase the effectiveness of praise and approval as conditioned reinforcers.

II. Goal—to transfer control of responding from the token system to other reinforcers such as teacher praise and grades.

III. Effective programs use in addition:
   A. Praise for appropriate behavior and ignoring disruptive behavior when tokens are not dispensed.
   B. Time out isolation, when intensely disruptive behavior occur.
   C. Systematic contingencies in the form of privileges are often applied throughout the day.
   D. Children following the rules are the ones who get to help the teacher, to be first in line, choose an activity etc.
   E. Praise, privileges and tokens are not administered for achieving an absolute standard of performance but for improving behavior or for maintaining a high level of acceptable behavior.
   F. If a child is hurting another child – withdrawal of all social attention and loss of the opportunity to earn tokens by isolating in a time out is suggested.
   – CATCH THE CHILD BEING GOOD!
   – FOCUS ON BEHAVIOR WHICH IS AN IMPROVEMENT AND REINFORCE IT!

IV. Instructions for introduction of token program.
    A. Prior to the explanation of the token economy to the children, a list of rules should be written on the chalkboard and left there while the program is in effect. (The rules worked out with the teacher can be: stay in seat, raise hand, quiet, desk clear, face front, and work hard.)
    B. Explain to the children that they will be rated on how well they follow the rules. A paper will be attached to their desks, and every rating period the teacher will put a number from 1 to 10 on their paper. The better a child follows the rules the higher the number he will receive.
    C. By earning points in this way, the children will be able to win prizes. They must have a certain number of points in order to win a prize. Show the children the prizes and explain that 10 points earns a prize from this box (show an example) and 25 points earns a prize from this box. Do not let the children handle the prizes.
    D. Emphasize that they will not receive prizes every day, and that sometimes they will have to collect points over two or more days in order to obtain prizes. However, they will be told how long they have to work to earn a prize.

V. Instructions for operation of token program.
    A. Each day before the rating period, go over the rules with the children. Point out that they can earn prizes, tell them how many points they must have to win different types of prizes, and then show them some of the prizes they can win.
    B. When rating a child, point out the rules he followed in order to receive the point he did. "I'm giving you 8 points because . . . . , I'm not giving you 10 points because . . ." Also indicate what behavior could be improved on to earn full points.
    C. At all times, except when prizes are being shown to the class or when the children are picking out the prizes

they have earned, the prizes should be stored in a location where the children cannot reach them.
D. Except for the first day of the token program, prizes should be given out at the end of the school day. On the first day give out prizes after the third rating period.
E. The children will be rated from 1 to 10 on how well they follow the classroom rules and behave in class. Rules can be modified or changed, but if this is done, notify the class and put the change on the chalkboard.
F. The value of the prize will be changed as the children are required to earn more points to win prizes. The number of points required will be indicated on the appropriate boxes.
G. A child can be very well behaved to earn the highest value prizes. Do not allow the children to try to talk you into giving them more points. Make a judgment and then explain that he earned only so many points, but he can earn more by behaving better.

VI. Categories for Identifying Child Behaviors
   A. Deviant Behavior
   Gross motor behaviors. Getting out of seat, standing up, walking around, running, hopping, skipping, jumping, rocking chair, moving chair, knees on chair. Include such gross physical movements as arm flailing, feet swinging, and rocking.
   Disruptive noise. Tapping feet, clapping, rattling papers, tearing papers, throwing book on desk, slamming desk top, tapping pencil or other objects on desk. Be conservative, note what you hear, not what you see, and do not include accidental dropping of objects or noise made while performing gross motor behaviors.
   Disturbing Others. Grabbing objects or work, knocking neighbor's books off desk, destroying another's property, throwing objects at another without hitting, pushing with desk. Only note if someone is there.
   Contact. Hitting, pushing, shoving, pinching, slapping, striking with objects, throwing object which hits another

person, poking with object. Do not attempt to make judgments of intent. Note any physical contact.

Orienting responses. Turning head or head and body to look at another person, showing objects to another child, attending to another child. Must be of 4 seconds duration to be noted and is not noted unless seated. Any turn of 90 degrees or more from desk while seated is noted.

Verbalizations. Carrying on conversations with other children when it is not permitted, calling out answers to questions or comments without being called on, calling teacher's name to get her attention, crying, screaming, singing, whistling, laughing, coughing, or blowing nose. Do not note lip movements. Note what you hear, not what you see.

B. Relevant Behavior

Time on task, e.g., answering questions, listening, raising hand for teacher attention, working at assigned task, reading.

Goal Oriented Behavior

I. Theory—All behaviors have a purpose. If the behavior meets the goals of the child, it will continue.
    Teacher—if you can't understand the behavior – think it doesn't make sense – you haven't figured out what the goal is.
    Child—Understands it's the only way for him to achieve his goal.
    To Understand—View the child subjectively – from his point of view.

II. Four Goals of Misbehaviors
    A. Attention getting
    B. Power
    C. Revenge
    D. Display inadequacy

Regardless of the goal – the child is convinced that his behavior is the most effective way for him to function in the group.

    A. *Attention Getting*
    If the child cannot become part of the group through a positive contribution, he seeks belonging through attention. He will try any method as long as he's noticed.
    – The child would rather be punished than ignored.

    B. *Struggle for Power*
    1. Child tries to show he controls others, refuses to do what he is told – this mean defeat.
    2. If the adult succeeds in showing more power and winning, the child becomes convinced of the value of power and is more determined to win the next time.

    C. *Revenge*
    A result of antagonism. Child finds his place in the group by being hated. He can no longer hope for power or attention. He becomes successful by being vicious and violent.

    D. *Inadequacy As a Goal*
    The child expects only failure. Uses inability to do something in order to escape participation.

III. Group Influences

Peer approval more important than teacher or family approval.
- A. *Teacher*
    1. Uses the group to put pressure on the child.
    2. Stimulate proper values – those that make the child acceptable to the group.
- B. *Group Goals*
    1. Constructive – Centered around cooperation.
    2. Destructive – These children have switched to unacceptable behavior, their concern for others is low, they don't identify with other children in the group.
    3. Develop Constructive Goals
        I. Remember the child has to find an acceptable place within the group. Take advantage of this by providing these children with jobs permitting them to cooperate in the functioning of the classroom.
        II. Child adjusts to the group.
        III. Child develops self-understanding from feedback from the group.
    4. Group solves common problems together.

IV. Leading A Group

We concentrate on individual needs and individual differences. We forget:
- A. We are dealing with an entire group as well as individuals.
- B. Use the group to your advantage, or it may work against you.
- C. Look at:
    1. How the group works.
    2. Who are the leaders
    3. Who are the isolates.
    4. What are the subgroups in the class.
    5. Behaviors you find disturbing as a teacher – how do other children in the class (group) react to them.
    6. If you are not aware of the different groups in the class – you can't influence their behavior.

- If you decide not to deal with the group relationships in the class and continue towards educational goals – you may be permitting the disturbing child to get the class cooperating with him instead of you.
7. It is better to have the children cooperating with one another than competing with one another.

POOR DISCIPLINE = INEFFECTIVE HANDLING OF GROUPS

8. If students problem solve as a group together, they become more interested in:
   - working together.
   - cooperating as a group.

This also satisfies their need to belong.

Teacher = Group Leader
1. Makes group aware of what they're doing – provides feedback.
2. Encourages effective communication within the group for solving tasks that have common interests.
3. Develops a cohesive group.

V. Sociogram—for identifying groups/isolates
   A. Provides a picture of group structures.
   B. Picture of relationships among students.
   C. Obtain data by:
   Asking students to write down the names of 3 class members they would like as companions for a specific activity (sit near them, work with them, go to a movie with, invite to a party, play with).
   D. Students should be allowed to work in the classroom groups of their choice.
   E. The results allow the teacher to work with the individuals and groups effectively.
      1. Identify leaders.
      2. Identify popular students (Stars).
      3. Identify those who are isolates.
      4. Identify whom isolates would like to be friendly with.

5. You may find the isolates do have friends.
6. You may find children exhibiting negative behaviors really do have friends in the class that could influence their behavior because the friends exhibit positive behaviors.
   F. Charting the data for the sociogram is shown below.

The status of each member of the class is shown at that particular time. Group and personal relationships tend to change and the changes can be recorded using this method.

Constructing the Sociogram
The sociogram consists of a group of circles, one for each member of the group, drawn on a large sheet of paper. The responses of the group are taken individually and arrows are drawn showing the members chosen by each individual.

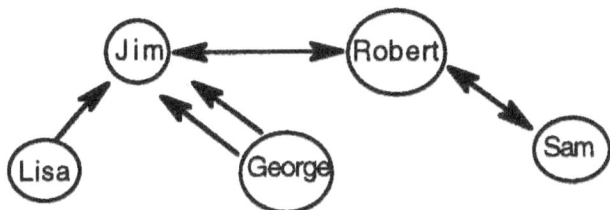

In the example above Jim is clearly the leader and Sam is the isolate except that Robert chose Sam. The 2-way arrow between Jim and Robert shows each one chose the other. Jim would be a good student to work with to organize the others and make him the leader of a group. Robert can be used to bring Sam into the group. Small groups in the class can identify cliques. Students identified in a class as isolates chosen by no one, can be students in need of counseling services.

Encouraging Students

I. Deterrents to overcome in order to encourage students

    A. *Obstacle*
       1. The autocratic teacher based on the traditional model of punishing, finding fault.
       2. Believing in the out-dated system of punishment and reward, teaching a lesson.

II. Encouraging all children
    A. Being a democratic and liberal educator.
    B. Let them get by with things without punishment and retaliation.
    C. Forget about using fear and intimidation to keep children in line.
    D. Build self-confidence and ego in children – if a child feels inferior or insecure he bolsters his ego by tearing others down. This makes him feel superior.
    E. Make everyone a winner.

III. Results
    A. Cooperative attitude and relationship between teacher and students, student and student.
    B. No contest for superiority or power.
    C. Students feel secure and supportive – are cooperative and constructive.
    D. Mistakes are not emphasized but successes are.

Remember to be sincere in praise.

Behavior Modification – A Process For Learning

I. Theory—Behavior is learned and modification is based on a cause – effect relationship. Modification includes techniques for changing behavior.

  A. Discipline—is the teachers responsibility.
  B. Why they don't want to learn?
    – Some don't want to learn.
    – Some don't want to learn what we want them to learn.
  C. Motivation
    Children must be taught to be:
    – motivated
    – curious
    – interested
    – to establish their own goals
  D. Why practice spelling—if child receives attention:
    – wandering around the room
    – writing notes in class
    – using pencil sharpener
  E. Rewards
    – Learning behaviors should provide rewards.
    – Adults don't pursue activities that are meaningless, difficult, and they think are a waste of time.
    – Children must be aware of the rewards of learning.

II. Teacher's Problem
  A. Making work task pleasurable.
  B. Developing child's capacity to work.
  C. Includes the process of teaching for delayed rewards over an increasing span of time.

III. Behavior—defined
  A. Anything a person does, says, or thinks that can be observed directly or indirectly.

B. Stimulus—response + techniques for changing behavior to behavior that is appropriate to the situation.

IV. Children:
    A. Work for things that bring them pleasure.
    B. Work for approval from people they care about.
    C. Change behaviors to avoid unpleasantness.
    D. Tend to repeat behaviors they have often repeated.

V. Discipline and Behavior
    A. Appropriate behavior
    B. Inappropriate behavior
  *C. To eliminate inappropriate behavior:
      1. Find the reward and eliminate it. It's different for every child.
      2. Behavior that is unrewarded will extinguish.
      3. Observe the child carefully to determine the reward he is receiving for his inappropriate behavior.

VI. Example
    Three children talk during classtime, finally teacher sends them to principal's office.
    Student # 1—This is exactly what he intended—he wanted to be punished.
    Student # 2—Liked making the teacher angry. He knew he was upsetting her and he enjoyed it.
    Student # 3—Didn't care about the teacher or the principal – he did care about student # 1 & 2. Every time this student talked, they listened.
    Result—Principal tells them to be good and not talk and returns them to class and they continue to talk even more, upon their return.

VII. Explanation
    A. Teachers who have one explanation for all maladaptive behaviors are usually ineffective (ie):
      1. The thing they need is a paddling.
      2. All those children need is a little love.

3. They need a decent place to live.
4. They need someone to understand them.

B. Why its not effective?
1. It's not differentiated – children don't fit the same category.
*2. THE ONE THING THAT CHILDREN EXHIBITING INAPPROPRIATE RESPONSES DO NEED IS A TEACHER WHO CAN FIND THE REWARD.
THAT IS KEEPING THE BEHAVIOR ALIVE?
3. IF THE REWARD CAN BE FOUND AND COMPLETELY ELIMINATED, THEN THE BEHAVIOR WILL GRADUALLY EXTINGUISH – IF CONSISTENCY IS MAINTAINED.

VIII. Results of eliminating the reward
1. Behavior initially gets worse.
2. Behavior then gets better because the student originally learned the behavior to get what he wanted.
3. When the reward is abolished, first he tries harder, then realizes there is not a reward so it extinguishes.

IX. How to eliminate undesired behavior
A. Only tackle one behavior at a time.
B. Make a list and put in an hierarchy with what is most important at the top of your list.
C. Make up a set of rules for the class regarding the behavior as well as a contingency (reward the desirable behavior).
1. Rewards should be:
    – known
    – tangible
    – close enough for students to want them, be desirable to them, and be considered a reward by the students.
2. At the beginning it is better to give too much reward than not enough.
3. Get the students winning as soon as possible.
    – tokens exchanged for prizes

4. Rewards can be HELD up to the class at the beginning of the day so students can choose which one they are working for that day.
    a. Teacher goes over the rules:
        I.   sit quietly during class
        II.   raise hand before we talk
        III. we stay at our own desk unless getting permission
    b. Teacher tries to catch a child being good and reward with tokens.
5. Suggestions for rewards—M&M's, juice, cold cereals.
6. Teacher can start the day with each child getting some cold cereal and telling children "we will have another party if everyone is quiet while I count to ten" (teacher then counts quickly making sure they win.) Then she distributes more and says "if everyone is quiet for 5 minutes we'll have another party. If someone talks – you say "Oh I'm sorry Joe talked before our time was up; now we will not get to have a party. Maybe tomorrow we can have one if everyone is quiet."
    – the teacher doesn't get angry at Joe—he receives the disapproval of the class—there's no payoff from the group.
    – teacher can choose to give the cereal to the quiet children and not to Joe.
7. Group approval – disapproval is very effective, when activities are given or denied, contingent upon the behavior of all students – the students will take the responsibility for the discipline.
X. What is a reward?
    Whatever the student is motivated to work towards.

Reinforcement Teaching

I. Shaping student behavior by restructuring the environment so students can receive approval/disapproval reinforcement contingent on appropriate/inappropriate behavior.
    A. If a student knows exactly what's expected of him, and he wants to do it, then he probably will do it.
    B. The teacher structures the reinforcements so that the student will do what the teachers expect of him.
    C. Five techniques used in structuring contingencies:
        1. Approval (rewards).
        2. Withholding of approval – withholding rewards (hope)
        3. Disapproval (punishment).
        4. Threat of disapproval (fear).
        5. Ignoring.
    D. Advice for teachers
        1. Use approval as much as possible.
        2. Next withholding of approval.
        3. Ignoring as the third in line of hierarchy.
    E. Positive approaches are more effective.
        1. Teacher should not be permissive.
        2. Punishment may be needed at times but try not use it.
    *3. Rewards come after the behavior.

II. Structure Activities By Time
    A. For contingent rewards/punishment to be effective:
        1. They must take place immediately following the behavior.
        2. The teacher must decide beforehand what the contingencies will be.
        3. Correct deviant behavior before it gets full—blown.

    *Initial stages of control by the teachers are most important.

    B. Structure rewards by deciding how long children can remain "good" and reward them at the end of the "good" period. You have to catch them being good and try to lengthen this time gradually. Thereby getting the student to wait longer periods of time and still exhibit appropriate behavior.

III. Consistency—If behavior is partially reinforced it is difficult to extinguish.
   A. Gambling reinforces partially – you win often enough to keep playing until you lose in the end.
   B. If you threaten to send a child to the office 3 times and don't, he doesn't expect to be sent the fourth and fifth time.
   C. You must think about the contingencies, structure them in your mind, make the rules, and follow through.
   D. If you break the rule and don't follow through, you have taught the child how to break the rule.
   E. IT ALL TAKES TIME BUT REMEMBER:
      1. If behaviors can be learned, they can be unlearned or relearned.
      *2. Punishment may stop a behavior but it does not teach appropriate behavior.
         a. A child who is hit because he hits with a spoon – will not learn correct etiquette. He learns not to use a spoon.
         b. A child punished for his bad writing – will not learn to write correctly he may stop writing.

IV. HOW TO . . .
   A. Pinpoint the behavior that is to be eliminated and its replacement. Make it observable and measurable in your mind – otherwise you will never know it you've succeeded.
   B. Record the behaviors to be eliminated in a hierarchy as to how often they occur. Take one at a time.
   C. Contingencies—Set up in your mind what your personal responses will be towards the inappropriate behavior when it occurs.

* Remember when you ignore it, it will get worse before it gets better.

EXAMPLES OF APPLYING THE PRINCIPLES

Bothering teacher at desk: Students unnecessarily at teacher's desk. Teacher ignored all children who came to desk-made no eye contact, said nothing. Teacher recognized only those children who raised hands at seats. Occurrences of students at teacher's desk steadily decreased. After two weeks, daily average between zero and one.

Inappropriate pencil sharpening: Teacher noticed two children going to pencil sharpener, then five, then entire class. Teacher got up from desk, gently removed sharpener bin, told children she would read a story if they completed work during next twenty minutes. They did – she did. A pleasant day.
Note: A teacher must catch a problem immediately.

Teasing other children: Disruptive behavior. Isolation—A coat rack and bookcase were arranged in back of classroom, making small isolation cubicle for child. Child sent to this "time-out place" for ten minutes every time he disrupted class.
Disruptive behavior steadily decreased. After nine isolations (four during the first day) disruptive behavior dropped.
Note: This child's teasing behavior was probably producing "payoff" from class (laughing, complaining, attending).

Material not put away – Large FRIDAY BOX in classroom. Each student given responsibility for own materials—individually labeled. Materials not put away went in Friday Box. Friday Box opened half-hour weekly – (on Friday) *only then could articles be recovered.*
After second week of Friday Box, littering decreased to three incidents weekly.
Note: This procedure seems effective in all situations and at all age levels. The amount of material not taken from the box that is allowed to remain week after week provides a good indication of its worth to the litterer.

Disruptive classroom behavior: Disruptions recorded by teacher. Disruptive behaviors ignored: appropriate behavior rewarded. Boy kept after school for extreme disruptions and sent home on later bus. This put child with students he did not know and withdrew peer attention. Correct behaviors reinforced by teacher praise and peer-approval (continuously in beginning, more infrequently later on). Also, job of chalkboard monitor followed appropriate behavior. Disruptive behaviors initially increased as payoff withdrawn. After initial rise, maladaptive behaviors progressively decreased and were eliminated by end of third week.

Aggressive hitting: Teacher complained boys were "out of control" during outside play periods (five children hurt in one week). Large punching bag dummy with red nose installed on playground. No noticeable decrease in human hitting – six children hurt during week. Dummy punched frequently, especially in nose. (Actually, boys fought each other to take turns at dummy).
Punching dummy removed. Individual boys isolated for duration of play period when observed hitting another child. After five days (seventeen isolations), hitting completely eliminated.
Note: Hitting, like other behavior, is learned. It is not a mystical entity deep inside everyone's system waiting to be released. The more children are reinforced for hitting, the more they will hit. Some people even develop a curious "self-fulfilling prophecy" in this regard. They sincerely believe that if they could just hit something they would feel much better. Thus, when frustrated, they hit something and, sure enough they feel better.

Bad Attitude: Child continued maladaptive responses just a little past point of instruction. Thus, when teacher said, "Stop talking," he did but continued *almost* to point of being disobedient. When teacher said, "Do not pick the flowers," he picked leaves. When she said, "Come here," he walked very slowly. When she said, "Quiet down," he did – still slightly louder than the group but not so loud as to receive punishment. This child (like so many others) delicately balanced upon the "edge of propriety." Punishment seemed not quite warranted, and reward seemed ridiculous.

Teacher set up short lesson using *vicarious modeling*. Three names not duplicated in classroom were written on board. Class presented with a new word, attitude. Teacher paired names with the new word:—"George has a bad attitude: Sam has an all right attitude; Tommy has a good attitude. When their teacher tells these boys, "Lets all pick up the mess," George tries to get out of work or hides his mess in the desk, Sam cleans up his own mess – only his own –, but Tommy cleans up his own mess and then helps other children." The teacher talked through two such specific examples, then let children say what they thought George, Sam, and Tommy would do. (Children are usually very correct in these assessments, especially as they describe their own problems.) Teacher made several praising comments, stating: "I liked Tommy the very, very best." She then asked problem boy whom he would want for a friend. (The teacher now had a word, attitude, that she could use to describe this boy's behaviors in specific and general contexts – "That's a good attitude Cort.") She now began rewarding good attitudes instead of being frustrated at not being able to find responses to deal with this child.

Child in question changed "attitude" when rewarded for proper verbal and motor behavior.

POSITIVE REINFORCEMENT YOU CAN USE

I. WORDS

Yes	Correct
Good	Excellent
Neat	That's right
Nice	Perfect
O.K.	Satisfactory
Fascinating	How true
Charming	Keep going
Delightful	How beautiful
Brilliant	Wonderful job!
Fine answer	Fantastic!
Uh-huh	Terrific!
Positively!	Swell
Go ahead	Beautiful work
Yeah!	Tasty
All right	Marvelous!
Nifty	Exciting!
Exactly	Pleasant
Of course	Delicious
Cool	Fabulous!
Likeable	Splendid
Outstanding work	Thinking
Of course!	

II. SENTENCES

That's clever.
I'm pleased.
Thank you.
I'm glad you're here.
That's a prize of a job.
You make me happy.
That shows thought.
We think a lot of you.
You're tops on our list.
That's good work.
Remarkably well done.
You're very pleasant.
That shows a great deal of work.
Yes, I think you should continue.
A good way of putting it.
I like the way (name) explained
    it.
That is a feather in your cap.
You are very friendly.
That's an excellent goal.
Nice speaking voice.
That's a nice expression.
It is a pleasure having you as a
    student.
That's interesting.
You make being a teacher very
    worthwhile.

You are improving.
You're doing fine.
You perform very well (name).
That's very good (name).
I'm so proud of you.
I like that.
This is the best yet.
That's the correct way.
That's very choice.
You do so well.
You're polite.
Thinking!

III. RELATIONSHIPS

Nice things happen to nice children.

That is very imaginative.

You are worthy of my love.

That will be a great benefit to the class.

I admire it when you work like that.

That is original work.

I appreciate your attention.

You've been a fine credit to your class.

I commend your outstanding work.

We are proud to honor your achievement.

That was very kind of you.

You catch on very quickly.

Obedience makes me happy.

That deserves my respect.

You demonstrate fine ability.

That was nice of you to lend her your _____.

I wish you would show me and the class how you got such an interesting effect.

I like that – I didn't know it could be done that way.

Permission granted.

That's a good job – other children can look up to you.

Let's watch him do it.

He accepts responsibility.

That was a good choice.

My, you have a nice attitude.

Now you're really trying.

Keep working hard.

You've improved.

Your work appears so neat.

You're a good person.

If at first you don't succeed try, try again.

Thinking.

Show this to your parents.

I know how you feel – should we continue.

I'm happy your desk is in order.

Why don't you show the class how you got the answer.

I agree.

Let's put this somewhere special.

I'd like this in my own house.

IV. WORDS AND SYMBOLS WRITTEN: APPROVAL

Bravo
Improvement
Fine
Good
Neato
Very Good
O.K.
Passing
*
X
√
Thoughtful
100 %
Good paper
Very colorful
☺
Well done
Great
WOW!
A-1
Perceptive

Good work

Correct
+
Satisfactory
Nicely done
Very concise
Complete
A, B, C, D
Oʘᴏ— Enjoyable
Excellent
Outstanding

{Colored pencil marking}
Superior
Congratulations
Yeh
Show this to your parents
{Honor Rolls}
For display
🕶 stamps

☺

V. RULES

In formulating rules, remember to:
1. Involve the class in making up the rules.
2. Keep the rules short and to the point.
3. Phrase rules, where possible in a positive way. ("Sit quietly while working," instead of "Don't talk to your neighbors.")
4. Remind the class of the rules at times other than when someone has misbehaved.
5. Make different sets of rules for varied activities.
6. Let children know when different rules apply (work-play).
7. Post rules in a conspicuous place and review regularly.
8. Keep a sheet of paper on your desk and record the number of times you review rules with class.

VI. EXPRESSIONS: APPROVAL

Facial
Looking
Smiling
Nodding
Grinning
Raising eyebrows
Forming kiss
Opening eyes
Laughing (happy)

Widening eyes
Wrinkling nose
Blinking rapidly
Giggling
Whistling
Cheering
Slowly closing eyes
Chuckling

VII. EXPRESSIONS: APPROVAL

Bodily
Clapping
Raising arms
Shaking fist
Signaling O.K.
Cocking head
Skipping
Rubbing stomach
Thumbs up
Shaking head
Shrugging shoulders

Grabbing
Bouncing
Dancing
Stroking motions
Opening hands
Flipping head
Taking fast breath
Expansive movement
Hugging self

Circling hands through air (pointing to hand/finger to face, eyebrows, eyes, nose, ears, hair, forehead)

VIII. ACTIVITIES AND PRIVILEGES: APPROVAL

A. Individual
Leading students group
Representing group in school activities
Displaying student's work (any subject matter)
Straightening up for teacher
Putting away materials
Running errands
Caring for class pets, flower, etc.
Collecting materials (papers, workbooks, assignments, etc.)
Choosing activities
Show and tell (any level)
Constructing school materials
Dusting, erasing, cleaning, arranging chairs, etc.
Helping other children (drinking, lavatory, cleaning etc.)
Reading a story
Exempting a test
Working problems on the board

Individual continued

Answering questions
Outside supervising (patrols, directing parking, ushering, etc.)
Classroom supervision
Omitting specific assignments
First in line
Assisting teacher teach
Leading discussions
Making gifts
Recognizing birthdays
Grading papers
Special seating arrangements
Responsibility for ongoing activities during school holidays (pets, plants)
Decorating room
Presenting hobby to class
"Citizen of the Week" or "Best Kid of the Day"

B. Materials

Storybooks	Pencil holders
Picture for magazines	Stationery
Collage materials	Compasses
Counting beads	Calendars
Paintbrushes	Buttons
Papier-mâché	Pins
Book covers	Pictures
Crayons	Musical instruments
Coloring books	Drawing paper
Paints	Elastic bands
Records	Paper Clips
Flash cards	Colored paper
Surprise package	Pets
Bookmarkers	Flowers
Seasonal Cards (valentines, birthday)	Chalk
	Clay
Pencil sharpeners	
Subject—matter accessories	

C. Food

Jawbreakers
Lemon drops
Chocolate creams
Sugar cane
Cake
Crackers
Lemonade
M & M's
Candy canes
Popcorn
Candy corn
Peanuts

Milk
Sugar-coated cereal
Marshmallows
Apple
Gum
Potato chips
Juices
Raisins
Lollipops
Candy kisses
Popsicles
Fruit

Animal crackers
Crackerjacks
Ice cream
Candy bars
Soft drinks
Cookies
Life savers

D. Playthings

Toys
Perfume
Cartoons
Kaleidoscopes
Flashlight
Headdress
Rings
Striped straws
Playground
equipment
Tape recorders
Badges
Pins
Ribbons
Balls
Bats
Toy jewelry
Blocks
snakes

Stamps
Whistles
Bean bags
Jumping beans
Wax lips and teeth
Masks
Straw hats
Banks
Fans
Silly putty
Toy musical
instruments
Tokens (points)
Grab bag gifts
Birthday hats
Cowboy hats
Boats
Miniature cars

Puzzles
Play dough
Combs
Dolls
Comics
Dollhouse
Balloons
Jump ropes
Makeup Kit
Trains
Commercial games
Stuffed animals
Toy guns
Pick-up sticks
Marbles
Jacks
Yo-Yo's

Plastic toys (animals, indians, soldiers)
Money (play, real, exchangeable)
Household inexpensives (pots, coffee cans, all sizes of cardboard boxes)

IX. EXPRESSIONS: DISAPPROVAL

Frowning
Curling lip
Lifting eyebrows
Looking at ceiling
Furrowing brows
Smirking
Lowering eyebrows
Shaking finger or fist
Wrinkling mouth
Squinting eyes

Staring
Wrinkling forehead
Puckering lips
Nose in air
Wrinkling nose
Pounding fists on table
Laughing
Shaking head
Turning away
Gritting teeth

POSITIVE IS BETTER

Remember as a teacher, you have so many positive and effective resources at your fingertips, you don't have to resort to the negative and primitive measures.

Develop positive responses.

Monitoring Student Behavior

I. Traditional Approach
Teacher's desk in front of class can see all students.

In Actuality
Students are monitoring the teacher's behavior. They are aware when you are watching them and when you are otherwise occupied.

II. Alternative Approach
Teacher's desk in rear of class facing the backs of students monitoring students behavior.

In Actuality
Teacher is monitoring students behavior and they are unaware of teacher being occupied with other things.

III. Monitoring/Assisting Individual Student Seatwork
Teacher bends over work at student desk to provide assistance.

In Actuality
Teacher unable to see misbehaviors.

IV. Alternative Approach
Teacher deep knee bends at students' desk to provide assistance. Gives the teacher the opportunity to just raise eyes to view the rest of the class. Try to position yourself at the desk in such a manner as to not have your back to the rest of the class. (May have to stand sideways).

Reality Discipline

Theory—People must be helped to realize their behavior is irresponsible and then need to be helped to make their behavior responsible—William Glasser.

A. Children are taught to identify behavior that hurts them or others and then make plans to solve the problem.
B. Children who learn to do this become responsible for their own behavior and learn self-control.
  1. A child who breaks a rule is asked:
     – What are you doing?
     – Why?
     – Is it helping you?
     – Is it against the rules?
     – What will you do to change that?
  2. A teacher accepts no excuses, repeats questions again, sends students to time-out place to develop a plan to stop the behavior from occurring again.
     a. The plan includes steps for following it and consequences for failing to following it.
     b. The teacher can have input into the plan, but it is written by the students.
     c. After the plan is implemented student and teacher meet to evaluate if it's working.
C. Class Meetings—These are a must! Held in a circle at a specific time from 10-45 minutes led by teacher or student, everyone encouraged to share, there are no wrong answers. Everyone expresses idea, opinions, and feelings on a variety of topics. Classroom meetings raise self-esteem, foster communication and problem solving, and increase moral reasoning, leadership, and listening skills.
  There are three types of meetings: open-ended, educational/diagnostic, and problem solving.
  1. Open-ended meetings are ones in which students create their own fantasies and explore imaginary problems.

2. The educational/diagnostic meeting is one where a topic being studied by the students is discussed to see what they know and don't know, and to determine further interest. You can then use that information to make decisions about what would be essential to cover and what would be most relevant.
3. Problem solving is one where the class focuses on a real problem and offers solutions. (This may included problems of fellow classmates.)

Classroom meetings make a class much more caring and a democratic community. There is definitely a sense of shared responsibility and increased participation among all. Most students have not been involved in such a setup and need time to open up and share their feelings, without feeling threatened.

At the first meeting you should establish rules. Have the group set them up because they are more apt to respect and follow them when they have a say in the formation. Students usually come up with rules such as: raise hands, but only after the person is done speaking (otherwise the speaker feels rushed); no talking or negative comments; and stay on the subject being discussed. Rules should be simple, and there should be no more than five: otherwise, there will be too many for students to remember. The teacher's role is to make sure rules are followed. He/she must help develop listening and speaking skills, and encourage students to participate and react to the opinions of others.

D. Learning Centers—Activities and materials for individual student growth where children are actively involved in learning, working at different rates, and using a variety of styles.
Allows for:

- movement in room for restless students
- attention span to remain high
- increase in noise level for actively involved students

E. Occupying Students Completing Work Early.
    If you give them additional work they consider it "not fair". Plan for options they enjoy and can choose from. Below is a list of suggestions:
    - projects—anything the child is interested in and would like to learn more about (great for research)
    - silent reading
    - creative stories
    - finish up other work not completed
    - on certain days—games
    - drawing
    - tutor slower children
    - choice of learning centers
    - run errands, do room chores
    - correct papers
    - manipulatives
    - puzzles
    - arts and crafts
    - work on lesson to present to the class

F. Noisy while Lining up—Call students by rows, colors, birthday, or any type of listening activity. When you have a group lining up at a time, you can control the class and maintain peace and quiet. Students lined up should be quiet or sent back to their seats. You should let the class know from day one what your expectations are for hall lining behavior, as well as the consequences when these expectations are not met.

    For the first couple of weeks, if students are noisy in the hall, have them go back to classroom and start all over. Noisy halls show disrespect for others! Make a game out of walking in the hall. Students could pretend to be mice who don't want the cat to hear them, or they could be soldiers. Appoint captains for the week, and have those leaders control the noise in the halls. Don't get in the habit of saying – "Shhh!" This is not really a way to establish control. The end of the line is usually noisier that the front, walk at the end. You can see everything that is going on in front. Have students stop at the corners, just to make sure they are being quiet and they are keeping together, as a group. Responsibility is the key to self-discipline.

G. Class activities when teacher completes all activities early—When there are a few extra minutes at the end of the school day or class period some suggestions are listed below.
   1. Flash cards – math skills, spelling, vocabulary words.
   2. Simon Says – listening skills.
   3. Map skills – Have students come find states, rivers, mountains, on maps either at their desks, or on a room map.
   4. Review spelling words – Pick individual students to spell words, or use slates where everyone can write the words (slates are effective for quick review).
   5. Read to students. (When reading, use different voices for the characters and vary the tone – children love it!)
   6. Pantomime reading vocabulary words.
   7. Create a poem about the day.
   8. Around the world using math facts – Begin by pairing two students against one another. Show a flash card; the first one to answer correctly moves on. (Winner is the student who makes it past all other students, therefore has gone "Around the World.")
   9. Mum ball – Students sit on top of their desks and pass a nerf ball to one another. (Rules – No talking, the person throwing the ball must throw so that the other person can catch it. No one can move from

the desk top; otherwise they are out and must sit in their seat.)

10. Spell-O – Put all the spelling words on the board; students write down any four. Choose one student to go to the board and slowly begin checking off one word at a time (any order); students at their seats check off any time a word is given on their papers. When all four words are called the student stands up and says "Spell-O". He/she gives the list to the person at the board and must correctly spell each word of the four words; if the student does this, then he/she can be the person at the board.

11. Do stretching exercise or aerobics.

12. Moral discussions – Make up a story and have students discuss solutions. (Example: You find a wallet on the playground. Inside is a $10.00 bill, just the amount you need to finally get the bike you have been saving to get for months. No one is around to see you if you take the money. You really want the bike! What do you do?)

13. Sing action song – Hokey Pokey, Bingo or even camp songs.

14 Make lists – How many different things are made of circles, squares? Give a word and ask students to come up with as many different words as they can which mean the same or opposite thing.

15. Seven-up – Seven students stand in the front of room while the rest of the class is seated with head down, eyes closed, and one hand fisted with the thumb up on desks. The seven students go among classmates, each one pushing a thumb down. They return to the front of the room, and the teacher says, "heads up." Those students that were touched must stand and try to guess who touched their thumb. If they guess correctly, they replace the person who touched them. The game continues until everyone has their turn to participate, or until allotted time is over.

16. Describe things or people in the classroom and have students guess what or who it is.
17. Start with a sentence (Example: "I went to the store and bought . ."). Each student must add something and repeat what everyone else has said previously.
18. Brainstorm various topics such as current events (discuss things students have heard on TV/radio), school problems, suggestions for upcoming projects or units.
19. This is similar to Wheel of Fortune—Box out a number of letters on the board. Ask one student at a time for a letter; the one who gives a letter has a chance to guess the character (usually from a book that is being read at the time). You fill in the letters, and the student who does guess can do another character on the board.
20. Concentrate game – Students list things by the alphabet. The first student begins with letter "a" (e.g., apple), the next one repeats "apple" and gives a word that begins with "b", and so on. Different categories can be used.
21. Baseball – Can be used with flash cards, spelling words, or other subjects. Divide the class into two teams. Flash a card to the student, and he/she is given three seconds to answer. If the student answers correctly, he/she goes to "first base" (a designated spot). The next student follows the same procedure and goes to first, while first goes to second, and so on. An incorrect answer is an out, three outs and the other team is "up". Score by getting a player "home."
22. Basketball – This also can be used with math facts, or spelling words. Divide into two teams. The first player up is flashed a card or given a spelling word to spell and use in a sentence. A correct answer earns a point. If answered correctly, the player gets to throw a nerf ball into a wastepaper basket. If the

basket is made, it is worth two points. The teams rotate twice.

23. Guess my word – Place the beginning letter of the word you want students to guess on the board. Divide into two teams. Give a definition of the word from the dictionary and allow teams to guess what the word is.

24. What's the missing word? – Put a sentence on the board, but leave out a word. Put only the beginning letter on the board. Divide into two teams and have teams come up with a word that could be used correctly in the sentence.

25. Computer games.

26. On three-by-five cards, write questions to important concepts covered, pass out and have students answer. If you write answers on the back of the cards, students can use these as individual reinforcement.

27. Write a number on the bulletin board, have students stare at it for 5-10 seconds, then erase. Have individual students guess the number. (Do 8-10 digits for third graders.)

28. Begin a story and then go around having each student make up the next part when it's their turn.

29. Make cards to cheer up people at nursing homes or hospitals. If time permits have students write a quick note to go along with it.

30. Students usually love to draw. Give them a topic and let them go to work. (Example: Draw me a picture of a house you would like to live in. Draw me a picture of a pet you would like to have. Draw something you would like to invent.) You could also have students add a few sentences why or describing their drawing.

Logical Consequences

Theory—The consequence is arranged by an adult but is the result of the students' own act. It should be a corrective procedure rather than a punishment. (Dinkmeyer, Dreikurs)

I. Punishment—Is resented by a student and the student refuses to accept the adult authority. The student tries to find ways to defeat the adult. Punishment is ineffective in deterring misbehaviors. It's a power struggle.

II. Logical Consequences
    A. Teaches students to deal with the consequences of their actions, and develop to maturity as healthy human beings.
    B. Does not show the power of the teacher as the authority figure.
    C. Invokes the rules of society.
    D. The consequence is related to the misbehavior (punishment is usually not connected to the misbehavior.)
    E. The student must see clearly the relationship between his act and the result of his behavior. Otherwise he will view the consequences as a punishment.

III. Presupposition of logical consequences
    A. Acts are judged good or bad by society.
    B. This does not change the value of the student as a human being.
    C. Misbehaviors are mistakes.
    D. The adult has the responsibility to point out the misbehavior without labeling the child as good or bad.
    E. Punishment makes the child feel he has no value.
    F. Logical consequences avoids making a judgment about the child.
    G. Unpleasant consequences as a result of a child's act, teaches him to avoid the act in the future.

H. An important factor – It doesn't make the child feel he is subject to the whim of an authority figure which he cannot control.
I. A logical consequence gives the student the choice of deciding for himself whether or not he wants to repeat the act.
J. Use a friendly voice when invoking a logical consequence. Tone of voice is a gauge for open or underlying attitudes.
1. A critical or punitive voice can turn a consequence into a punishment.
2. A harsh voice does not imply friendliness but demands, causes anger, pressure or retaliation (which you will want to avoid).
3. Friendliness has to be genuine, after all you are helping to socialize the student so he can be accepted by society.
4. Be careful—don't get personally involved with the student's act and think it is against you.
It is not.

IV. Examples of Logical Consequences
A. Two children are scuffling on the playground instead of participating in the same activity the other children are.
1. *Punishment*—Teacher tells them to sit on bench for the rest of the class period.
Result—Children are antagonized by the teacher's command they don't see the corrective intent.
2. *Logical Consequence*—Teacher says "I see you don't want to play the game like the rest of the group; therefore, please sit on the bench until you're feeling ready to play properly."
Result—Teacher removes herself from the authority role by relating the result of the childrens' action to what they are doing. This also tells them that their return to the group is possible if they alter their behavior. Chances of teacher success are greater using this approach. What the teacher says should be in a tone that is unemotional and matter of fact.

It's not the teacher's fault they are on the bench, its the result of their behavior.

B. A student had the habit of constantly tipping his chair back in class. He had once fallen back on the floor. He continued this behavior for attention.

Student Goal—Attention getting

1. Teacher asked student if he preferred to lean back in chair or sit like rest of children. Boy said he preferred to lean back. Teacher put a book under front legs of chair so the boy was leaning back in an uncomfortable not dangerous position. He was told to keep this position until he decided to sit properly. Boy finally removed the books and didn't tip chair anymore during the rest of the year.

C. Verbal Misbehavior

When attention getting is the child's goal:

- A simple "I know you're there" by the teacher to the student who is acting out for attention usually startles the student and extinguishes the behavior. This may have to be repeated a few times in the beginning.
- Another day—when this same student enters the classroom the teacher can say "Good morning, I know you're here today." This may eliminate the attention getting behavior that day.

D. One boy was always late coming in after recess causing him to miss explanation of his seat work. He was told it wasn't fair to the other children for the teacher to take class time to explain to him because he wanted extra play time.

1. Logical Consequence—Next time he was late he was not given an explanation and couldn't do the work. When he asked what to do, he was told he would be given an explanation as soon as the others were dismissed. Then he had to finish the work before he left. He was not late again.

2. Teacher did not reprimand the boy, just refused a special service during the class hour. As he knew beforehand what would happen if he came in late, it was up to him

to decide what he preferred, to cut his play time or finish his work later.

V. Use of Group Consequences

For misbehavior of an entire class – to be used when the teacher is attempting to provide class instruction.

A. Call class to order and say "There has been so much noise here I'm not sure whether you really got what I was trying to get across so let's take out our papers and have a little test." Then present the most difficult questions you can think of. When grading papers—give as many low grades as possible, don't put grade in book. This can be effective if the students are concerned about their grades. *Do not give repeated warnings regarding behavior prior to giving the test otherwise the entire exercise will be received as a punishment for the class by the students.*

B. Not following instructions

Many times this is for attention getting. Sometimes after giving directions the same 4 or 5 students always say they don't understand. Tell class, "I will give instructions for this exercise two times". If students say they don't understand, tell them you gave the instructions twice. Say no more – they probably got the instructions (unless of course they were not understandable by the students). You can write them on the board and if asked simply reply "see for yourself" and point to the board.

C. Private conversation between students during class time.
   1. Look in their direction—if they don't stop . . .
   2. "name and name you seem to have something to say to each other, something that can't wait. You two go out into the hall and tell each other what you want to say—and when you are through you may come back."

D. Student constantly out of seat, leaning on desk, doing work from half-standing position. "Would you rather stand or sit while doing your work? It makes no difference to me which you prefer." If student says he prefers standing then tell him "Then you no longer need your seat and we can take the chair out of the room." Remove the chair from the room for the remainder of the day. The next day at the beginning of the class period ask the student if he prefers sitting or standing. If he says sitting return the chair.

E. Preventing Fights

Tell the class "If anyone fights he is telling us he doesn't like to play with us; therefore, he should leave and sit by himself until he feels he can join the game without fighting." If he continues fighting, he needs more time to think about it, so if necessary, he can sit out the entire recess. The more time he fights, the longer he has to leave the game; he also realizes that no matter how quickly be comes back, his place is lost.

F. Class not starting on time

If class is noisy after the bell rings, which is the time the class is to start – sit quietly and say nothing, wait for them to be quiet. Note the amount of time it takes. It's a good idea to look at your watch – it gives them a clue. When it is time for lunch or dismissal, and the bell rings – go on with the lesson and excuse them late (approximately the period of time it took them to get started earlier in the day.) The next day should take them less time to get settled—so only keep them this shorter period of time.

* **Remember**—You are doing students a service using the logical consequences approach – they are learning acceptable behavior and the consequences resulting from their actions. You are not punishing them, you are not angry, frustrated, or annoyed – this is just the way it is!

Questions And Answers

I. Tips for Getting Class Attention
   1. Whisper.
   2. Turn the lights off.
   3. Start a patter by clapping.
   4. Use a bell.
   5. Raise your hand and have everyone else do the same.
   6. Stand in front of the room with your arms crossed and don't say a thing.
   7. Play the listening game by saying "If you are listening, touch your nose, touch your stomach, touch your arm" and so on. Just say, "If you are listening, you are sitting up straight, your hands are folded, and your mouth is closed."
   8. Start giving directions in normal tone of voice, gradually getting softer and softer. Children will have to stop speaking in order to hear you.

II. Best time for sharpening pencils
   A. Before the lesson starts.
   B. Right after lunch.
   C. Tell them this is the rule and they should sharpen 2 at a time so if one breaks they have another one.

III. "Why do we have to learn this?"
   Check your lesson objectives, tell students what they are. Tell them the relevance for later in life. Sometimes teach the lesson and ask students why they think it was taught.

FURNITURE ARRANGEMENT 1

FOR EXTREME BEHAVIOR PROBLEMS

With all students facing the walls – teacher may monitor behavior by being in the center of the classroom and walking around.

Students do not know when they are being monitored by a teacher as the teacher moves around the room monitoring student work.

This is more effective if the teacher wears sneakers.

FURNITURE ARRANGEMENT 2

FRONT OF ROOM

TRADITIONAL ARRANGEMENT

If you prefer a traditional classroom arrangement – have students facing forward but teachers desk in rear of room. This aids the teacher in keeping an unobserved eye on students while they are doing their seatwork.

DURING DIRECT INSTRUCTION—It is best to make sure you address students from varying parts of the room – sometimes either one side or the other side or from the rear of the room. When a teacher constantly speaks to students from the front of the room, students on the sides and sitting in the rear feel neglected, are not in touch with the teacher, and often misbehave. This helps.

```
TEACHER'S
DESK
```

REAR OF CLASSROOM

FURNITURE ARRANGEMENT 3

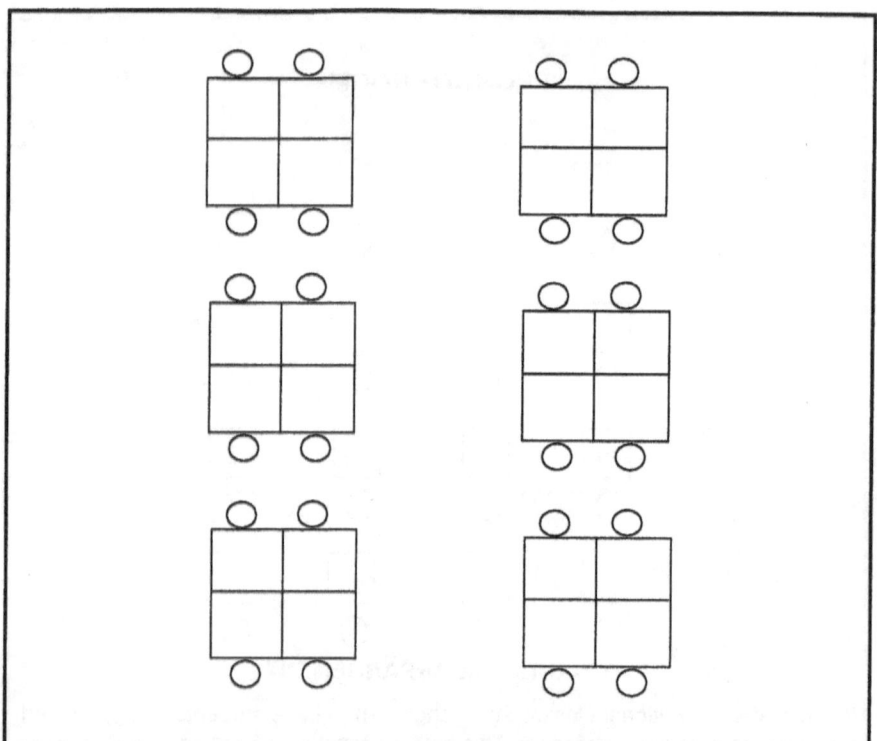

GROUP DISCIPLINE

If furniture is arranged in groups of 4 (6 if you have tables), it fosters group work by students, and can be used to pressure peers into behaving.

1. Dismiss students by group; which behaves best leaves first. Peers will pressure the misbehaving students to behave. You say nothing.
2. Can be used in going to recess, lunch, any other activity, class, reward etc.

FURNITURE ARRANGEMENT 4

GROUP INTERACTION

If you want to foster group interaction/communication/decisions, this can be a good arrangement for the group decision process.

Again it is important for the teacher to address the group from varying positions of the room. There is no front of the room therefore all students are periodically in close proximity to the teacher

www.ingramcontent.com/pod-product-compliance
Lightning Source LLC
Chambersburg PA
CBHW021301280526
45784CB00005B/2469